MY INDOOR Garden

MY INDOOR
Garden

CAROL LERNER

Morrow Junior Books
New York

To my fellow members of the La Porte County Master Gardeners Association

Watercolor and pencil were used for the full-color illustrations.
The text type is 14-point Sabon.

Copyright © 1999 by Carol Lerner

Published by Morrow Junior Books
a division of William Morrow and Company, Inc.
1350 Avenue of the Americas, New York, NY 10019
www.williammorrow.com

Printed in Hong Kong by South China Printing Company (1988) Ltd.

10 9 8 7 6 5 4 3 2 1

Library of Congress Cataloging-in-Publication Data

Lerner, Carol.
My indoor garden/Carol Lerner.
p. cm.
Summary: Discusses how to care for plants indoors, including such aspects as light, temperature,
humidity, pests, diseases, equipment, and how to choose and grow your own plants.
ISBN 0-688-14753-4 (trade)—ISBN 0-688-14754-2 (library)
1. Indoor gardening—Juvenile literature.   2. House plants—Juvenile literature.   [1. Indoor gardening.
2. Gardening.] I. Title.   SB419.2.L47 1999   635.9'65—dc21   98-18929   CIP AC

CONTENTS

AN INDOOR GARDEN—
ALL YEAR ROUND

Imagine a window full of lush green plants on a gray winter day—a whole shelf of them in a variety of shapes, sizes, and textures, some with bright flowers and striped leaves adding splashes of color.

Most houseplants came from tropical regions that never have freezing temperatures. These plants are evergreens, which means they keep their leaves in all seasons. Although indoor conditions cannot match the climate of a rain forest, with care you can keep these plants beautiful and growing for many years. This book will tell you how.

Once you own plants, you may discover that what you enjoy most is creating more of them. Small pieces of plants, called cuttings, or slips, can be used to grow whole new plants. Some species will multiply with very little encouragement. Others require a bit more effort. But most houseplants can be increased by using one of the basic techniques described in this book.

When you have mastered these techniques, you will be able to increase your stock of the plants you own. You will also be able to enlarge your collection by asking other indoor gardeners for cuttings from their plants or by trading plants with them.

Or you can raise plants to give as gifts to friends and relatives. Gardeners have a long history of sharing their enjoyment of plants with others, and you can become a partner in that fine tradition.

Happy gardening!

Hanging basket: wandering Jew
On the windowsill, from left
to right: begonia, chenille
plant, partridge breast aloe,
fishhook cactus, barrel
cactus, crown of thorns,
schefflera, croton, pothos.

THE NAMES OF PLANTS

Every known plant in the world has been given a two-part Latin name. The first part is the name of its genus—the group of closely related plants to which it belongs. The name of the genus is written in italics and is always capitalized. The second part of the name, also in italics but usually not capitalized, refers to that particular species of plant. The very common spider plant, for example, carries the scientific name *Chlorophytum comosum* (klor-oh-FY-tum koh-MOH-sum), which means "green plant with tufts." Every botanist in the world recognizes that plant by this Latin name.

Most of us simply call plants by their common names. But sometimes this is confusing because several different species may be known by the same common name, or a single species may have a number of different common names. (Spider plant is also known as airplane plant.)

This book will refer to plants by their generally accepted common names, if they have one. On pages 46–47 you will find scientific names of all the plants mentioned here.

Sometimes you will see an additional word or two, written in single quotation

spider plant
Chlorophytum comosum
'variegatum'

marks, as part of a plant name. This refers to the name of a cultivar, which is a plant that has been cultivated to preserve features that are slightly different from the plant that bears the species name. For example, *Chlorophytum comosum* 'variegatum' (vare-ee-ah-GAY-tum) is a cultivar of *Chlorophytum comosum* that has green leaves edged with white.

GETTING STARTED

LIGHT

Before you start collecting houseplants, you should decide where you will keep them. Windowsills, or shelves or tables placed very close to windows, will provide the best natural light.

The amount of light reaching the plants will depend upon the size of the window and—especially—upon the direction it faces. Windows that face the south receive the most sunshine unless trees or buildings block the sun's rays. In the southern parts of the United States, south-facing windows may actually be *too* bright for most plants.

Farther north, it is unlikely that plants will get too much sun during the winter months, but they may need to be shaded by a thin curtain or moved to a window with less direct sunlight in the brightest days of summer. Leaves that wilt in the middle of the day or leaves that develop brown patches and start to shrivel are signals that a plant is getting too much light.

A great number of plants do best in east- or west-facing windows, where the sun shines on them for only a few hours and they receive indirect light for the rest of the day. But even windows that look to the north and never receive direct sunlight may offer enough daylight for some.

If you can use windows that face in two or more directions, you will be better able to care for your plants' light needs. Plants from shady windows can take a turn in the sun for a few weeks, and the ones that occupy your brightest locations can move into shade during their dormancy, or resting period. (See "Dormancy," page 10.)

Since light from windows usually comes from just one direction, turn the pots from time to time so the plants don't become lopsided as they grow toward the sun.

SUNLIGHT WITHIN A ROOM

The amount of sunlight entering a room drops off quickly with greater distance from the window. Plants placed a few feet within a room receive only a small fraction of the light reaching the windowsill.

DORMANCY

Almost all plants enter a resting period, known as *dormancy*, at some time of the year. The plant stops growing. It may look a little limp and faded. If it is a flowering plant, it stops producing new buds. In some species, the change is dramatic: The leaves of amaryllis and cyclamen turn brown and collapse after their flowering period. Although life continues in their large storage organs, these plants appear to be lifeless for some months.

Dormancy is a normal part of a plant's yearly cycle, reflecting the seasonal changes in its native habitat. Most houseplants become dormant during our winter months. Dormant plants need little water and no fertilizer. See page 20 for information on plant watering during dormancy.

You will know the resting period is over when you see a flush of new growth.

Cyclamen in winter bloom

In summer dormancy

If you have no suitable window space at all, you can set up a corner with fluorescent lighting. Garden catalogs offer very expensive plant stands with built-in light fixtures, but with a little adult help you can rig up a low-cost lighting arrangement of your own.

Inexpensive light fixtures that hold two four-foot-long fluorescent tubes are sold at hardware and home supply stores. Even one lamp fixture hung above a shelf or table provides a good-sized growing space. If possible, the light should be hung so that it can be raised as the plants grow taller.

Your plants will receive the best light if the fixture is placed just four to eight inches above them. Since fluorescent tubes produce so little heat, they will not burn the leaves at this height. You can use two ordinary cool white tubes. These are least expensive and are often on sale. However, your plants will receive a wider range of light waves if you buy one warm white tube to use with one cool white tube. The type of light provided will be marked on the tube.

Plants must have regular periods of darkness too. Most people who garden under lights keep them on for twelve to fourteen hours a day. If your plants already receive some light from the windows, you can use the fluorescent lights for just a few hours each day. Watch your plants for guidance. If they become tall and "leggy," or if new leaves are small and pale, the plants need more time under the lights.

Nerve plant, wax begonia, Christmas cactus, and African violets growing under fluorescent lights

Wherever you grow your collection, make sure that the surface will not be stained by water. Plastic-coated shelf paper can protect a wood sill, shelf, or table. There are sure to be spills, no matter how careful you are when watering!

TEMPERATURE

Most houseplants thrive in temperatures that are in the range of sixty-five to seventy-five degrees Fahrenheit (eighteen to twenty-four degrees Centigrade), with a drop of five to ten degrees (three to six degrees Centigrade) at night. Less heat is better for some: A winter-flowering azalea or poinsettia will stay fresh and colorful for weeks if it is kept in a cool spot (fifty to sixty degrees Fahrenheit, ten to sixteen degrees Centigrade).

Don't assume that the temperature in your plant window is the same as the reading on the house thermostat, either in cold weather or in hot. Check the plant window temperature with an indoor thermometer. On severe winter nights, the window might transmit so much cold that you would need to put cardboard or newspaper between the glass and the plants to protect them from damage.

rubber plant   aluminum plant   baby's tears   prayer plant

HUMIDITY

Except for desert cacti and other plants that come from dry habitats, houseplants need generous amounts of moisture in the air. But heating our homes in winter results in indoor humidity that is much too low for most plants (or for us). Some homes have humidifiers on their heating systems that add moisture to the whole house. Or your family may plug in an electric room-humidifier. Even if you live in a very mild climate, your indoor winter humidity is likely to be well below the level that is ideal for tropical plants. You can measure the humidity level around your plants with an inexpensive hydrometer from the hardware store. Most houseplants do best with a humidity level between 50 and 80 percent.

It's hard to change the light and heat conditions in your home, but you can improve the humidity around your plants very simply. You will need some trays or pans (one to two inches deep is good) that will hold water. Disposable aluminum-foil pans used for pies and cakes or for roasts can be used. You will also need enough small pebbles to fill the bottoms of the pans with a layer about one inch deep. You can use small stones collected from the beach, or you can buy a bag of pebbles at a store selling aquarium supplies.

HOW HUMIDITY AFFECTS PLANTS

Water is absorbed by a plant's roots and carried up through the stem into the leaves. Some water is used for plant growth and some for the manufacture of food. Most of it passes out of the plant through tiny openings on the leaf surface called *stomata* and evaporates into the air. As the air surrounding the plant becomes warmer and drier, the rate of evaporation increases.

With central heating, the air in our winter homes can be as dry as the desert. To make up for the increased evaporation from the leaves, the plants must pump up more and more water from the soil. In drafty spots, the problem is worse: The flow of air over the leaves draws even more moisture from the plant. If it cannot draw up water fast enough to replace the loss, or if all the moisture in the soil is used up, the plant shows its distress by wilting.

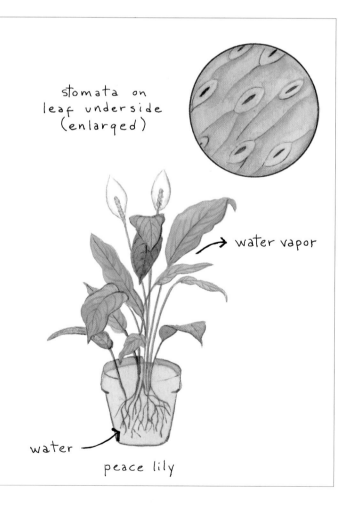

stomata on leaf underside (enlarged)

water vapor

water

peace lily

Group the pots together on the pebbles: This way each plant will benefit from the moisture given off by its companions. But leave some space between the plants too, so air can circulate around them. Then add water to the pan until the level comes to just *below* the bottom of the pots (not touching!) As the water in the pan evaporates, it raises the humidity of the air around the plants. Keep adding more water when you see that the level has dropped.

CHOOSING THE RIGHT PLANTS

Now that you have picked the best available place for your plants and have thought about the growing conditions there, you are ready to choose some plants for your indoor garden.

The most common houseplants are grown for their foliage—their attractive leaves. The leaves are boldly marked, or large and dramatic, or they have interesting shapes or textures. Some foliage plants never bloom in home conditions; if they do, the flowers are usually small and insignificant.

In general, foliage plants do well in bright indirect light, with little or no direct sunlight. But foliage plants with variegated leaves—that is, leaves marked with white or yellow or red or with different shades of green—usually need brighter light in order to retain their colors.

Houseplants grown for their flowers usually need lots of direct sunlight in order to bloom. The African violet is one of the exceptions to this rule: It can flower at any season of the year with no direct sunlight at all.

Succulent plants (see "Succulents," page 14) are special. Many succulents thrive in overheated apartments, even in dry air that would wilt other plants. Most need maximum light.

Some kinds of plants are not very demanding. They will do well in a variety of different light conditions. Others are fussy. Look at the chart on pages 46–47. It lists some widely available houseplants and the conditions they prefer.

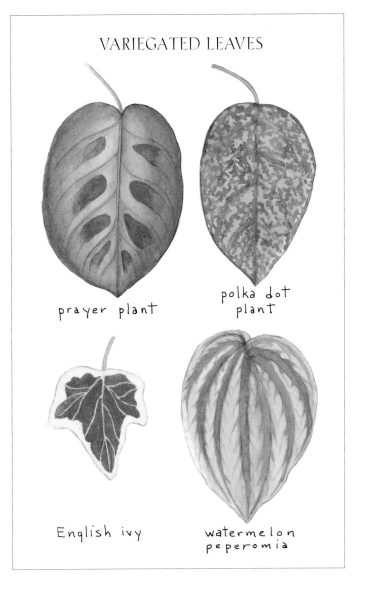

VARIEGATED LEAVES

prayer plant

polka dot plant

English ivy

watermelon peperomia

SUCCULENTS

A vast number of plant species grow in areas where water is scarce or undependable. In order to survive, these plants store a supply of water to carry them through dry periods. This ability to store water within stems, leaves, or underground parts is called *succulence*.

Desert cacti, such as the sea urchin cactus, store water in their prickly stems. Snake plants, burro's tail, and jade plants are succulent houseplants that hold a supply of water in thick, juicy leaves.

sea urchin cactus

snake plant

burro's tail

jade plant

SELECTING YOUR PLANTS

This book will tell you how to grow some handsome plants for your indoor garden by starting them from seeds or from small pieces cut from other plants. But since those procedures take time, you will probably want to begin with a few houseplants that are already up and growing.

Plants are available at a wide variety of stores—florists and garden centers, dime stores and supermarkets. But no matter where you buy your plants, take a close look at them before bringing them home.

Of course, you shouldn't even consider a plant that requires growing conditions you can't supply: It makes no sense to choose a desert cactus for a window with only an hour of daily sunshine. If the plants in the store have identifying labels, they may help you make your choices. The labels often give some information about light requirements and general plant care, as well as the name of the plant.

Look for young plants rather than full-grown ones. Small plants are much cheaper, for one thing. They are also more likely to adapt successfully to the change in growing conditions when you bring them home. And you will have the satisfaction of watching your young plant grow and reach maturity under your own care.

When you find a plant that appeals to you, look over every part of it. Are the stems strong and sturdy? Are the leaves green and fresh looking? Do you see healthy buds at the tips of the stems? Is the whole plant full and bushy, with a balanced shape? If you are buying a flowering plant, look for plenty of unopened flower buds. Finally, examine the plant closely for any signs of pests: Check along the stems, on the undersides of leaves, and in the angles where the leaves are attached to the stems.

If you are buying the plant on a cold day, ask the clerk to wrap it well before you take it out. Even a brief exposure to cold temperatures can kill tender leaves.

As soon as you get your new plant home, you will want to put it on display. Don't do it! Keep it away from any plants you already have. If your new plant shows no signs of pests or disease after a week or two, it's ready to take its place in your indoor garden.

An orchid cactus

CACTUS PLANTS FROM DESERTS AND FORESTS

A typical desert cactus lives in a place with a short rainy season; hot, sunny summers; and cool, dry winters. A smaller number of cactus species come from the Latin American rain forests. Many of these grow in trees, protected from the sun, sinking their roots into rotted plant matter that has built up in the angles of the branches.

The two groups of cacti need care that reflects their different natural habitats. As indoor plants, desert cacti need loose, well-drained compost and plenty of light. Forest cacti, such as the Christmas cactus and the orchid cacti (not related to the orchids!), require richer compost, indirect light, and more water and humidity.

EQUIPMENT

You will need a few pieces of equipment to care for your plant collection. You can probably find some of these things at home, so take a look around the house before you go out to buy them.

The essential items for routine care are:

- Saucers to go under plant pots (unless you are putting your plants on pebble trays).
- Watering can. Watering cans with long thin spouts make it easier to reach the right plant.
- Plant food. Concentrated liquid fertilizers are the easiest to use. (See "Reading a Fertilizer Label," page 21.)

Some useful items for routine care are:

- Mist sprayer. All-purpose plastic trigger sprayers are sold in hardware and garden stores. Use the sprayer to give your plants a shower bath in the kitchen sink. If you ever have problems with aphids (see page 23), blast them off with a hard jet of spray. You can also mist your plants to raise the humidity around them, but the effects don't last very long.
- Magnifying glass to help you spot tiny plant pests. Magnifiers that enlarge objects ten times (10X) are best.

Sooner or later, you will have to deal with the problem of plant pests. You will need:

- Cotton-tipped swabs.
- Rubbing alcohol (isopropyl alcohol).

When your plants outgrow their containers, or when you begin to grow your own plants (see pages 29–45), you will need additional items:

- Plant pots in different sizes.
- A plastic wash basin for potting, repotting, and soil mixing. (Do all your work inside this container to keep the mess off the floor.)
- Containers for growing seeds and cuttings. Any kind of shallow plastic or waxed cardboard container that is waterproof will do—margarine tubs, yogurt containers, cut-down milk or orange-juice cartons. Keep your eye on the kitchen garbage for useful discards. (Make sure you wash them well.)
- Transparent plastic bags to cover the containers of seeds and cuttings.
- Labels or markers to identify seeds and cuttings. Popsicle sticks are perfect.
- Rooting hormone, in powder or liquid form, for starting new plants from old ones. Some kinds of plant cuttings form roots more easily than others. Using rooting hormone will increase your chances of success. You can buy a small container in plant shops.

And finally, you will need a growing medium—material to fill the pots and nourish and support your plants. Because not all potting materials actually contain soil, they are referred to as composts rather than potting soils.

CLAY POTS OR PLASTIC?

Plastic pots are now much more common than clay pots. Plastic is cheaper, lighter in weight, more durable, and easier to clean. Unlike clay, no moisture is lost through the sides of these pots, so plants in plastic need less watering.

Many people prefer the appearance of traditional clay terra-cotta pots. Because it has more weight, clay may be a better choice for large, top-heavy plants that could tip over in a plastic container. Plants in clay do need more watering, but they are also less likely to suffer from waterlogged roots, because air and moisture can pass through the sides of the pot. This makes clay a good choice for cactus and other succulent plants whose roots need to dry out completely between waterings.

Old clay pots often become crusted with a layer of white mineral salts. To remove this, soak the pots in a mixture of vinegar and water (one cup of vinegar to one gallon of water) and then scrub them clean before using again.

COMPOSTS

Houseplants spend their lives in unnatural conditions, growing within the small space of a flowerpot. They can't spread their roots far and deep, as garden plants do. To do their best in such cramped quarters, the roots need special potting mixes.

Although some species of plants can live with their roots in water (see "A Water Garden," page 18), most plant roots will die unless they can obtain oxygen from air. Good potting mixes have a very loose texture, with countless little air pockets that provide oxygen for the tender root tips.

A WATER GARDEN

Some houseplants will grow in water without any compost at all. You might want to set up a window full of these plants. They will be especially attractive if you put your plants in colorful transparent glass containers. Colored glass will also keep the water from becoming too hot for the roots.

To make a water garden, put a few pieces of charcoal in the bottom of the container. (You can buy charcoal where aquarium supplies are sold.) Cover the charcoal with a few stones. If you are using plants that were grown in compost, wash off the roots before putting them into water. Mix some liquid fertilizer with water and fill the container with the mixture.

As the water level drops, keep adding water. And once a month, give the plant another dose of the fertilizer mixture.

These are some plants that will grow in a water garden—

Chinese evergreen	Swedish ivy
coleus	sweet potato
devil's ivy	ti plant
English ivy	umbrella plant
philodendron	wandering Jew
spider plant	

heart-leaved philodendron

Swedish ivy

English ivy

wandering Jew

Chinese evergreen

coleus

umbrella plant

If you use ordinary garden soil, your plants will have to struggle for survival. In an outdoor garden, vast numbers of little soil animals live underground, stirring and loosening the earth as they move. But soil in containers packs down every time it is watered. The air pockets it contained are squeezed out, and the soil itself becomes as hard as concrete. A shovelful of dirt from your yard could also introduce an army of pests and diseases to your indoor garden. Commercial potting mixes have received a heat treatment to kill off these harmful organisms.

Most potting mixes sold today contain no soil at all. The main ingredient is often peat moss or ground-up tree bark or some other kind of partly decayed plant matter. These mixtures usually have some added materials to keep the texture loose. Read the labels so you know what you're buying. These are some common additions:

- *Vermiculite* is made from a mineral, mica. The mineral is heated until the moisture within it turns into steam and the mica expands like popcorn. The spongy grains of vermiculite are gray-brown in color, and some of the grains have shiny surfaces. Vermiculite loosens soil texture and also absorbs water and minerals and slowly releases them back into the soil.
- *Perlite* is made by heating volcanic rock until it expands. Perlite, like vermiculite, keeps soil loose. The grains are white and lightweight and feel like ground-up Styrofoam plastic. They tend to rise to the surface of the potting soil when the mix is watered.
- *Coarse sand* improves drainage and creates pockets for air and water in the mixture.

Even with these added materials, potting mixtures sold in bags may be too dense for growing healthy plant roots. It is a good idea to loosen the compost further. You can buy a bag of vermiculite or perlite from the garden shop and mix in one cup for every two cups of potting compost. In place of vermiculite or perlite, you can use the same amount of clean coarse sand, which is much cheaper. But it must be *coarse*, with big grains. Sand is sold by companies that carry builder's supplies, but it usually comes in large sacks containing much more sand than you will need. Never use fine beach sand or sand from riverbeds, because the small grains will wash down and fill up all the air spaces in the compost.

Compared to composts containing soil, peat and other soilless mixtures contain few nutrients. Most of the plants raised by commercial growers are potted in soilless mixes that have been well fertilized to promote good growth.

Cactus and succulent plants (see pages 14–15) need very well-drained composts. Try growing them in mixtures containing equal parts of potting compost and coarse sand or perlite. If you don't mix your own, you can buy a bag of compost made especially for cactus and succulent plants.

PLANT CARE

WATERING

Watering is the most basic part of plant care. Unfortunately, there is no simple rule to tell you how much and how often to water. The amount of water a plant needs depends on the kind of plant; the size of the pot and the kind of compost it contains; the conditions of heat, light, and humidity that surround it; and even the season of the year.

However, here are a few points that will help you keep from over- or under-watering your plants.

Remember that most roots die if they are always in water and unable to absorb oxygen from air pockets in the compost. Wait until the top half-inch or so of compost is dry before watering your foliage plants. When they are dormant (see "Dormancy," page 10), give them even less water. Experts advise waiting until the dormant plant begins to show signs of wilting. Cactus and succulent plants, with their inner water storehouses, can go dry for weeks. In winter, you can wait until they start to wrinkle before watering them.

Of course, there are exceptions. If you have a winter-blooming plant, such as a Christmas cactus or poinsettia, it will need frequent watering until the end of the flowering period. A very few species of water-loving plants need to be kept wet *all* the time. An umbrella plant—if it is growing in compost rather than water—is one of these.

In springtime, with more daylight and higher temperatures, you will see spurts of growth. Those fresh new shoots and leaves signal the need for more frequent watering.

poinsettia

Your best guide on when and how often to water will come from looking at the plants themselves and learning to recognize their needs. Make it a habit to test the soil in each pot before you tilt the watering can. Poke your finger into the compost and rub a little dirt between your fingers. If you have a variety of plants, you will see that they use water at different rates. One may be bone-dry after a day or two, while another is still sodden. With practice, you will also be able to judge the dryness of the compost by lifting the pot and feeling its weight (dry compost is lighter).

When you decide a plant is dry, water it thoroughly—you want the water to reach down to the bottom of the pot, to encourage deep root growth. When water runs out through the drainage holes, that's the signal to stop. Empty the saucer after the pot has drained so the plant doesn't sit in water.

You can also water from below, placing the flowerpots in a pan of water and letting them soak until the surface of the compost feels damp. Drops of cold water on the leaves of African violet plants cause ugly brown spots. Bottom-watering takes much longer, but it guarantees a thorough soaking without wetting the leaves. If you use this method often, you will notice that a white deposit of mineral salts forms on the surface of the compost. Wash these salts away by watering from the top next time.

If you have forgotten to water a plant and discover that it has dried up because of the neglect, you might still be able to save it. Plunge the pot into a bucket that has water up to the level of the compost in the pot. When the compost is soaked through, let the pot drain and hope that you acted in time.

FERTILIZER

Plants need a variety of minerals for growth. These minerals, dissolved in soil water, enter the plant body through its roots. Since houseplants must fill all their mineral needs from the small ball of compost within their pots, you need to keep replacing the supply. You can do this by using a plant fertilizer.

Some of the minerals you add will be wasted—they will wash out of the compost into the saucer when a plant is watered. What remains in the compost can be used up in a few weeks' time by a plant that is making rapid growth.

But—just as with watering—do not apply fertilizer on a rigid weekly or monthly schedule. Watch your plants and learn to judge their changing needs. When they are resting and growth has slowed or stopped, they need no fertilizer. Most foliage plants growing in northern households need none from November through February. Fertilizer

READING A FERTILIZER LABEL

You will see a series of three numbers on packages of commercial fertilizer (5–10–5, 10–15–10, or 15–30–15, for example). These tell the proportions, by weight, of the three basic plant nutrients contained in the product. These nutrients are nitrogen, phosphorus, and potassium, and they are always listed in that order, alphabetically. Plants need nitrogen for green leaves, phosphorus for root growth and flowering, and potassium for disease resistance.

A fertilizer that is 10–15–10 contains 10 percent nitrogen, 15 percent phosphorus, and 10 percent potassium. The remaining 65 percent consists of fillers with no nutritional value.

Any all-purpose fertilizer sold for indoor use will provide good nutrition for your plants.

at this time can actually do damage: Since the plant has slowed down and cannot use the minerals for growth, the unused fertilizer will build up in the pot and may cause root burn.

Newly purchased plants usually come with so much fertilizer in their composts that they will need no additions for the first four to six months. When you repot a plant in fresh soil-based compost or in soilless compost that contains added fertilizer, you do not need to fertilize it for the next two or three months. And never feed a sick plant. Fertilizer is not a magical cure—it can actually kill an ailing plant.

Concentrated liquid fertilizers that are mixed with water before applying are inexpensive and easy to use. The package will give directions for mixing—how many drops or teaspoons of fertilizer to mix with each quart of water. Instead of following the instructions, make up a batch at half the recommended strength and start feeding every plant that is actively growing at two- or three-week intervals. After you see how each plant responds, you can decide to fertilize more or less often than that.

It is not always easy to figure out the cause of plant problems. Whatever the cause, plants have only a few ways to signal distress: poor growth; drooping, spotted, or falling leaves; poor flowering. Too much fertilizer or too little can result in the same symptoms! If your plants are in clay pots, one clear sign that they are getting too much fertilizer is the appearance of a white crust on the outside of the pot. In plastic pots, the excess fertilizer is trapped inside and doesn't show until the plant begins to weaken.

PESTS

If pests are eating your plants, you don't have to guess about the cause of the problem. Most pests can be seen if you look carefully. Some common ones, such as spider mites, are very tiny, so a strong magnifying glass comes in handy.

If you discover pests, pick up the pot right away and remove it from the other plants while you deal with the problem. And after you handle an infested plant, be sure to wash your hands so you don't carry the problem back to the healthy ones.

If the damage has gone too far, throw the plant away. Throw out the compost too. Before using the pot again, give it a scrub and soak it in a mixture of water and household bleach (nine parts of water to one part of bleach).

If you discover the pests before their numbers are too great, you should be able to save the plant. But of course, it is better to avoid the problem entirely if you can.

COMMON PLANT PESTS

APHIDS, or plant lice, are tiny pear-shaped insects that cluster on leaves and stems and suck plant sap. Adults are only one-eighth of an inch long and may be white, brown, green, black, red, or pink. Your first hint of aphids may be the appearance of a sticky substance called honeydew on the plant. A black or gray fungus called sooty mold may grow on the surface of the honeydew.

Give the plant a soapy bath (see page 24) to remove the aphids and rinse it with jets of clear water from a mist sprayer. There may be eggs in hard-to-reach places, so repeat the treatment every two or three days until the aphids are gone.

MEALYBUGS drink sap and leave honeydew too, but you are most likely to see small tufts of white "cotton" on stems and at the bases of plant leaves—in the angle where the leaf joins the stem. The insects are grayish white and wingless. They are usually small but may be up to one-fourth of an inch long.

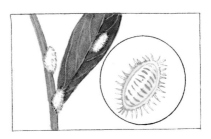

Remove them with a cotton swab dipped in rubbing alcohol.

SCALE INSECTS look like small bumps, flat or rounded, on stems and leaves—especially leaf undersides. They also leave telltale traces of honeydew. The insects may be brown, yellow, gray, or white, and up to one-fourth of an inch long.

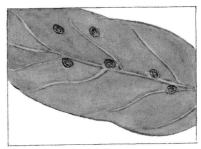

Remove the scale by scraping it gently with a fingernail or a tooth-pick. You won't see all of them the first time, so go back and inspect the plant every few days until you are sure it is clean.

SPIDER MITES leave webs of fine silk on the plants they infest. As they suck out plant juices, leaves turn dull and become marked with pale yellow dots. The mites are oval and may be green, yellow, red-brown, or colorless, but they are too small to see without magnification. If you hold a sheet of white paper under the plant and shake the leaves, you might see little specks crawling around on the paper.

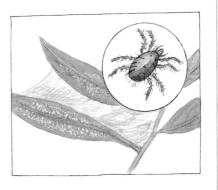

Spider mites thrive in dry air, so try to keep humidity high in winter. Give infested plants a soapy bath and rinse them with a hard spray. Be sure to hit the leaf undersides.

WHITEFLIES are tiny (about one-sixteenth of an inch) active moths that suck plant juices and leave honeydew behind. They rest on the undersides of leaves and fly off when disturbed. The young are usually on leaf undersides too: They look like flat greenish white scales and do not move.

It is hard to get rid of them. When the air is cool and the moths less active, you might be able to kill some by touching them with an alcohol-soaked cotton swab. Try giving the plant a series of soapy baths at five-day intervals.

GOOD HYGIENE

Get in the habit of looking over each plant whenever you check the compost for dryness, each time you water or fertilize, and even when you stop just to admire your collection. Pay special attention to the stems and the undersides of leaves.

Always pick off dead leaves or flowers: Rotting plant parts provide food for some insect pests. Frequent showers for plants that have smooth leaves will wash away unwelcome visitors and help to keep the leaves healthy. Wash plants early in the day so the leaves will be completely dry before temperatures drop in the nighttime.

You can wash small plants with a mist sprayer or under a faucet. Tilt the pot under the faucet so the stream of water strikes the plant but not the compost. Clean large plants by wiping the leaves with a soft damp cloth or by giving them a quick rinse under the bathroom shower.

An occasional soapy bath is a good practice. Mix a few drops of mild dishwashing detergent in a bucket of warm water. Cover the top of the compost with your hand or with a piece of plastic and swish the foliage around in the wash water. Then rinse the plant with clear water at room temperature to finish the job.

It is best not to wet the hairy leaves of plants such as African violets. You can brush dirt off the leaves with a very soft brush, such as a small paintbrush.

DISEASE

Like all living things, plants may sicken from disease—from infection caused by bacteria or by a fungus or virus attack. Good plant care is the best way to prevent illness, because healthy plants can resist infections. Sometimes overcrowding triggers the problem, because there is too little air circulation around the plants.

Disease spreads, so move a sick plant away from the others as soon as you see that there is a problem. Remove all the unhealthy stems, leaves, or flowers and discard them. If there's anything left, give the plant a soapy bath and a rinse. But don't return it to your collection until you are sure it has recovered. If in doubt, throw it away along with its compost. It's not worth risking the health of your other plants.

PINCHING BACK

Many plants become scraggly as they grow, with long stems and just a few leaves on each. To grow thick, bushy plants, learn the art of pinching back.

Pinch the growing tip of a stem between the fingernails of your thumb and index finger and nip it off. Make the cut just above a node—the growing point where a leaf is attached. And always pinch at a time when the plant is actively growing.

After the tip is removed, you can expect to see growth in two or more of the side buds on the lower parts of the stem. And after these side branches have grown new

Unpinched
avocado plant

Avocado branching
after pinching back

leaves, you can pinch their tips too, to encourage more bushiness.

Any plant that sends up its leaves directly from the soil line should not be pinched. This includes many ferns, the peace lily, African violets, and palms, as well as cactus and most other succulents. (In any case, you would never be tempted to pinch a cactus plant! See page 26 for the proper handling of cacti.)

WHY PINCHING WORKS

Plant growth is controlled by a group of hormones called *auxins* (AWK-sins), which are concentrated in the tips of growing stems. The auxins stimulate growth of the topmost bud, called the *apical* (APE-i-cull) bud, and—at the same time—prevent development of buds on the lower part of the stem (side buds, or *lateral* buds).

When the growing tip and its auxin supply are removed by pinching back, some of the lateral buds break out of dormancy and side shoots begin to grow from the stems.

apical bud

side bud

pinch here

Pinching back a coleus plant

REPOTTING

As a plant produces new stems and leaves, its roots are growing too. When its roots fill all the space inside the pot, the plant begins to signal that its roots need more room. Lower leaves turn yellow and die. You may notice that the plant seems to need watering constantly. One sure sign is the appearance of roots growing out of the pot's drainage hole. (By this time the plant is in urgent need of larger quarters!)

To inspect the roots, water the pot and wait at least a few hours. Then cover the surface of the compost with one hand, turn the pot upside down, and tap the rim against the edge of a table. Try to slip the rootball out of the pot. If it sticks, loosen it by running a spatula around the edge of the pot.

An overgrown root system will still keep the shape of the container when you slide it out of the pot. You will see white root tips growing all around the root ball. If the roots have coiled around and around within the pot, try loosening them with a fork. Clip off any dead roots and brown top growth with a scissors.

If your plant needs to be repotted, use a new pot that is just an inch or two larger than the old one. Determine the size by measuring the diameter of the top of the pot. Make sure the pot is clean. If you are using a brand-new clay pot, soak it in water until bubbles no longer rise from it.

The drainage hole of a clay pot needs to be covered in order to keep the compost from washing out. The traditional material is a few crocks—pieces of broken clay pots. You can also use a layer of gravel. The small holes in most plastic pots don't need to be covered.

HOW TO POT A SPINY CACTUS

Cactus plants grow slowly, so they don't out-grow their pots for years. But when the time comes to repot, use a clay pot, compost that drains well (see page 19), and special handling to protect yourself from the spines.

To pick up a cactus safely, fold a piece of newspaper into a narrow band that has three or four layers. Wearing leather gloves, wrap the band of paper around the cactus and move it into the new container. Use a spoon to fill the pot with compost and to level it around the base of the plant.

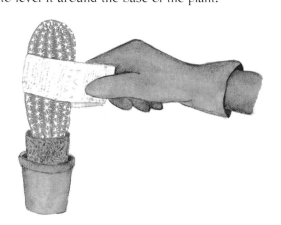

Add a layer of fresh compost and center the plant on it. The plant should be placed so that the top of its compost will be about half an inch below the rim of the pot. Then add more compost all around, pressing it down with your fingers so there are no pockets of air. *Don't bury the plant*—the new compost should come just to the level of the old.

Finally, water the plant and put it in a shady spot for a day or two until its roots begin to grow into the new compost.

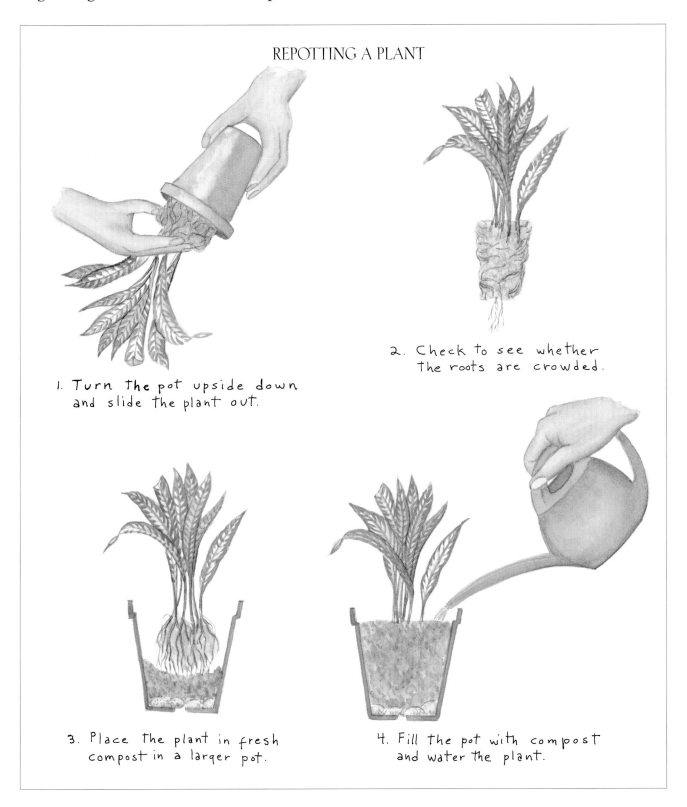

REPOTTING A PLANT

1. Turn the pot upside down and slide the plant out.

2. Check to see whether the roots are crowded.

3. Place the plant in fresh compost in a larger pot.

4. Fill the pot with compost and water the plant.

VACATION TIME

If you leave home for a week or less, your plants will probably manage very well without you. Just give them a thorough watering before you go and move them out of direct sunlight.

For longer trips, the ideal solution is to have a friend or relative be your plant-sitter. Or, if your collection is small, perhaps you can take it to a friend's house during your absence.

If you have no one to take care of your plants, you can leave them behind safely by enclosing them in plastic bags.

First give the plants a good soaking and check them for insects. After the pots drain, put each one in a transparent plastic bag. If necessary, poke some thin sticks into the compost to keep the plastic from resting on the leaves. Seal each bag with a rubber band and then place the plants in a spot where they will have good light but no direct sunshine. The sealed bags will retain enough moisture to keep the plants healthy for three weeks or even longer.

Left to right: shamrock plant, kalanchoe, Boston fern

Over the summer, most plants (but not African violets) will profit from an outdoor vacation too. A shady yard or patio or a spot along the north side of a building is just right—but never full sun. Your plants will lose moisture more quickly in the open air, so check them often to see if they need water.

Bring them back inside when summer is winding down. If you bring them in a month or six weeks before the first fall frosts, they can get used to being indoors before the heating season starts. But before returning them to the house, check each plant for insects once again and give them a shower under the hose.

GROWING YOUR OWN PLANTS

PLANTS FROM SEED

Seeds seem like the obvious way to start new plants. They certainly make good sense when you want a great many plants of one kind. You can raise dozens for the price of one seed packet.

But most indoor gardeners want to enjoy a variety of different plants. If you want only one or two pots of any single species, it doesn't seem sensible to buy a whole package of seeds. In any case, garden centers rarely sell seeds of tropical houseplants. You would have to go to specialized catalogs to find these.

Still, there's a real satisfaction in producing a beautiful plant from a tiny seed—if you have the patience. In some cases, you may have to wait weeks after planting until a seed sprouts. And it will take months of care before your seedling becomes a size-able plant.

If you want this challenge, you can find good choices on any seed rack in the spring. Some common outdoor plants make perfectly good houseplants: Coleus, petunia, and impatiens seeds are widely available and easy to grow. If you start the seeds in summer, these plants will provide colorful leaves and flowers to brighten your winter display of foliage plants. You don't have to plant the *whole* packet of

petunia

impatiens

seeds—just enough for three or six plants, or as many as you have room for. (Remember that not every seed will sprout, so plant some extras.) Put the leftover seeds in a tightly sealed jar and store it in a cool, dark place to use when you would like more plants.

Clean containers are important in seed-starting. Young seedlings may be killed by a fungus disease called damping off: Their tender stems rot at the bottom and collapse. If you use containers that held plants before, scrub them well.

Choose shallow containers (about two inches deep) for tiny seeds such as those of coleus. If you are planting in juice cartons or other recycled grocery containers, punch drainage holes in the bottom.

Fill the container with a half-and-half mixture of peat moss and vermiculite or clean coarse sand and pat it gently to level the surface. Dry peat moss is hard to moisten, so water the mix a few hours before planting to allow time for the water to soak in. You can use a commercial compost instead, but be sure to buy a package that is labeled as a seed-starting mixture.

Scatter tiny seeds over the top of the compost, leaving space between them, and pat the surface lightly so the seeds make contact with the compost. Water the container by setting it in a pan of warm water until the surface of the compost feels damp.

Let the newly watered container drain well. Then label it with the name of the plant, and the date, and seal it inside a transparent plastic bag. Keep it warm but out of direct sunlight. Temperatures in the seventies (twenty-one to twenty-six

1. Scatter the seeds on the compost.

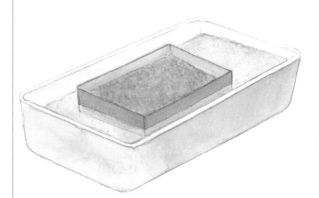

2. Water the seed container from below.

3. Drain the container and enclose it in a plastic bag.

4. After the seeds sprout, remove the bag and thin the plants.

5. Lift each seedling and move it to its own pot.

degrees Centigrade) are best, so perhaps you can place the container on top of a radiator or next to a hot air duct to keep the compost warm. But make sure neither heating unit is too hot. Temperatures over eighty-five degrees (twenty-nine degrees Centigrade) can kill seeds. If you see heavy beads of water dripping down the inside of the bag, remove the bag and put it back on inside out.

When sprouts appear, take off the bag and gradually move the container into direct sunlight. Cut out any crowded seedlings at the level of the compost with a nail scissors. Keep the compost moist but not soggy.

When the seedlings have three or four true leaves (see "Seeds and Seed Leaves," page 32) and are large enough to handle, you should transplant them into individual pots filled with potting compost. Use the tip of a pencil to lift each seedling, and grasp the plant by a leaf (not by the stem). Poke a hole in the new compost—just large enough to hold the root system of the seedling—and plant it. Firm the compost all around the stem with your fingers so the roots will come into contact with the potting material, and water the seedling.

After a day or two in the shade, move the young plants into the sun and watch them grow!

SEEDS AND SEED LEAVES

Within even the smallest seed is an *embryo*—a small undeveloped plant—and a supply of nourishment to support its early growth. A *seed coat* wraps around the embryo, protecting the contents until conditions are right for sprouting.

One part of the embryo is a *cotyledon* (cot–ih–LEE–dun), or seed leaf. Depending upon the species, the embryo has one or two seed leaves. When the embryo breaks out of the seed coat and begins to grow, the seed leaves of some species stay underground. In others they emerge as the first "leaves" of the seedling. In many plants the seed leaves contain the food that was stored in the seed, and they wither away as the seedling uses up the food. By that time the plant's *true leaves* are ready to take over the job of making food for the growing plant.

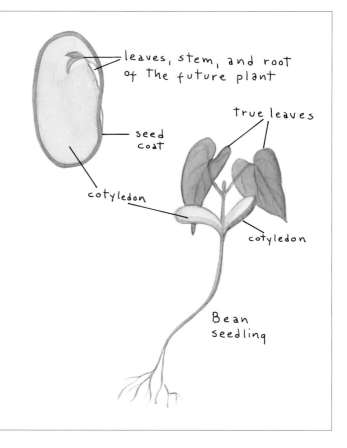

leaves, stem, and root of the future plant

seed coat

cotyledon

true leaves

cotyledon

Bean seedling

You can also try raising plants from some of the seeds you find in fruits from the grocery store. Seeds from any kind of citrus fruit (orange, grapefruit, lime, lemon) grow into attractive houseplants (but don't count on harvesting any fruit from them). A big avocado pit or seeds from a pomegranate are other possibilities. Even coffee beans will grow if you plant some that have not been dried by roasting.

Fairly large seeds, such as citrus or pomegranate, can be planted in four-inch pots in a mixture of one part potting compost to one part perlite or vermiculite. You can plant six to ten seeds in one container. As a general rule, cover the seeds with compost to a depth about twice their diameter. Then handle the pots of seeds just as described above.

The big pit of an avocado can be planted in its own four-inch pot in regular potting

A young lemon plant

compost. Bury the pit halfway with the pointed end up. Or start the avocado in a jar of water with the bottom half of the pit submerged. Move it into potting compost when its root is about an inch long.

GROWING AN AVOCADO PLANT FROM SEED

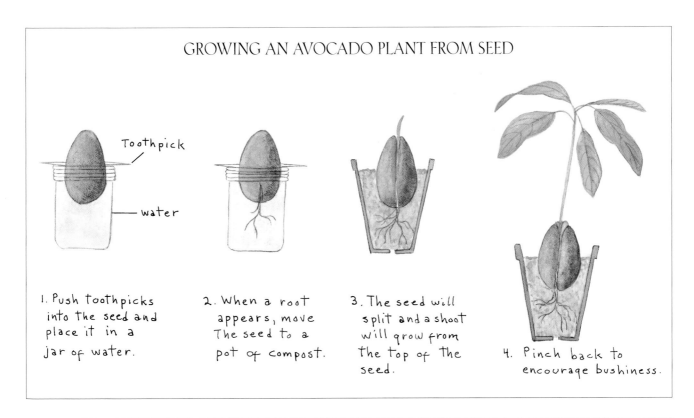

Toothpick

water

1. Push toothpicks into the seed and place it in a jar of water.

2. When a root appears, move the seed to a pot of compost.

3. The seed will split and a shoot will grow from the top of the seed.

4. Pinch back to encourage bushiness.

PRETREATING SEEDS BEFORE PLANTING

Some seeds need special handling before planting. Plants from temperate climates—that is, climates with cold winters and warm summers—produce seeds in the fall. In nature, the seeds spend winter on cold, damp ground before sprouting the following spring. The seeds of some species, such as apples and daylilies, will not sprout unless they first experience a cold period.

Putting seeds through an artificial winter period is called *stratification* (plant nurseries used to bury seeds in layers—strata—of moist soil or sand outdoors over the winter). You can experiment with seed stratification by using seeds from a grocery kiwi fruit, a plant that is a native of China.

Remove some of the small black seeds from the plant's center and squeeze them in a paper towel to remove the pulp. Then fold the seeds in a clean paper towel, wet the towel, and squeeze out the extra water. Put the towel in a plastic bag with some damp sand, peat moss, vermiculite, or more layers of moist towel. Label the bag, date it, and store it in the refrigerator. (Be sure to tell everyone in your house what the bag contains so they won't disturb your seeds.)

After six weeks, plant the seeds in starting compost and treat them like any other newly planted seeds.

kiwi fruit, cut open to show the seeds

TWO PLANTS (OR MORE) FROM ONE

Plants produce their seeds as the result of a sexual union: when male pollen grains come together with the ovules—the future seeds—inside a plant ovary. If pollen from one plant reaches the ovules of another, the seeds will contain a mixture of the genes of the two parent plants. Plants that grow from the seeds are not perfectly identical to either one of the parents.

It is also possible for a new plant to grow from roots, stems, or leaves—the non-sexual, or vegetative, parts of plants. If the tip of a wild raspberry bush bends to the ground and takes root in the soil, it will produce a new, independent plant. Potatoes are usually grown by planting a small piece of potato rather than a seed.

When a new plant grows from a vegetative part of a plant—whether naturally or by human efforts—the process is called vegetative propagation. Plants grown this way are clones: They are identical in every way to the plant they came from.

Not every part of a plant will take root and become a new plant, but most house-plants can be multiplied by some form of vegetative propagation. It is a quick and easy way to increase your plant collection.

When you experiment with vegetative propagation, use the same kind of compost that was recommended for seed-starting unless you are potting plants that already have roots. Rooted plants can go into your usual potting compost.

Simple Layering

Simple, or ground, layering is a way of encouraging a new plant to grow on a piece of stem that is still attached to the parent plant. After the new plant develops, it is separated from the parent. You can try this technique with any kind of climbing or trailing plant—plants with long stems that bend without breaking. Ivy, kangaroo vine, philodendron, pothos, and wax plant are good candidates. Layering works best in spring or early summer, when the plant is in active growth.

To propagate a plant by layering, choose a long, healthy stem. Select a point on the stem a few inches back from the tip and ask an adult to make a cut with a sharp

wax plant   kangaroo vine   English ivy

knife at that point. The cut should go *halfway* through the underside of the stem. Dip the cut area in rooting hormone and hold it down to moist seed-starting compost in a separate pot. Use a hairpin or paper clip to peg it down.

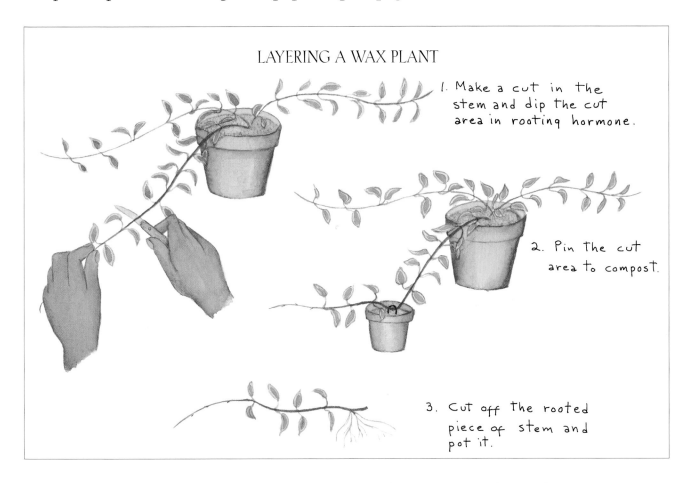

LAYERING A WAX PLANT

1. Make a cut in the stem and dip the cut area in rooting hormone.

2. Pin the cut area to compost.

3. Cut off the rooted piece of stem and pot it.

The parent plant will nourish the stem tip, but you must keep the starting compost moist. After a few weeks, roots should form and new leafy growth should appear from the tip of the buried stem. If you are not sure whether the stem has rooted, you can lift it up to take a look. If roots haven't formed yet, bury the stem again and give it more time. If you see roots, you can cut the stem from the parent plant and move it into a pot containing potting compost.

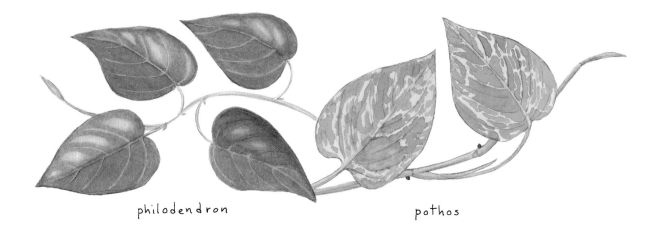

philodendron   pothos

Plantlets

A few kinds of houseplants present you with miniature copies of themselves, ready to be planted and grow. The spider plant and strawberry begonia send out long runners with plantlets at the tips. The piggyback plant and the species of *Kalanchoe* (kal-un-KOH-ee) called mother-of-thousands produce tiny plants on their leaves. All of these are easy to multiply.

To propagate a plantlet, pin it to the starting compost, just as in stem layering. Keep the compost moist. In a few weeks, when roots have formed, separate the new plant and move it into a pot containing potting compost. In propagating the mother-of-thousands, remove a leaf from the plant and place it on regular potting compost.

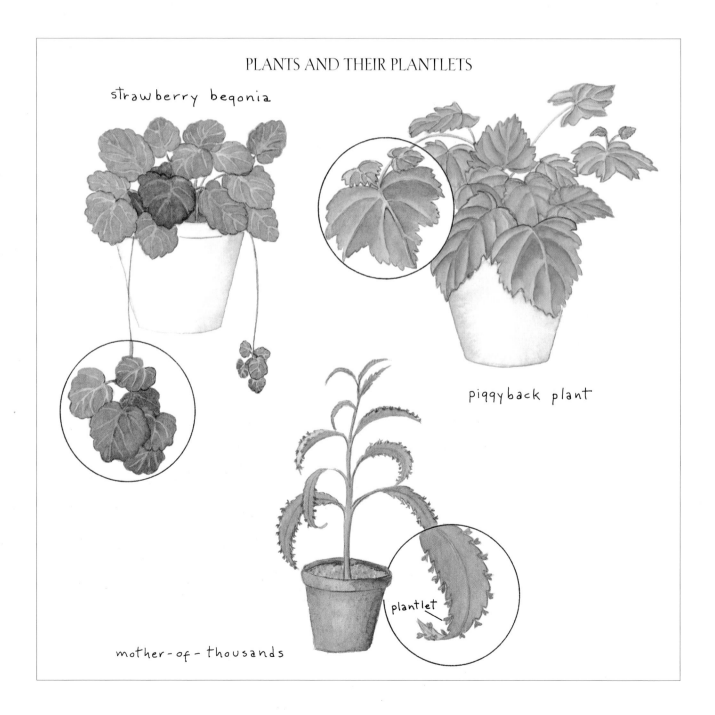

PLANTS AND THEIR PLANTLETS

strawberry begonia

piggyback plant

plantlet

mother-of-thousands

Division

If you grow African violets or succulent plants such as aloe or echeveria (ek-uh-VEER-ee-uh), you will occasionally discover a small companion plant growing in the shadow of a larger one. Many plants increase in number by producing offsets or suckers, a natural kind of vegetative reproduction. Offsets grow from buds at the crown—the part of the plant at the surface of the soil or compost. Suckers grow from below ground, from roots or underground stems. Both can be separated from the parent to become independent plants. Like layering, dividing plants is most successful during the season of active growth.

Dividing a plant will be messy, so begin by knocking the plant out of the pot over a dishpan so that the compost does not get all over (see page 27). The young plant will be connected to the parent. Ask an adult to cut them apart cleanly with a sharp knife. After they are separated, pull the plants apart very gently.

When you divide the two, you may see that the offset or sucker already has roots. In that case, you can plant it in ordinary potting compost. If there are no roots, put it in seed-starting compost and enclose the pot in a clear plastic bag until roots develop.

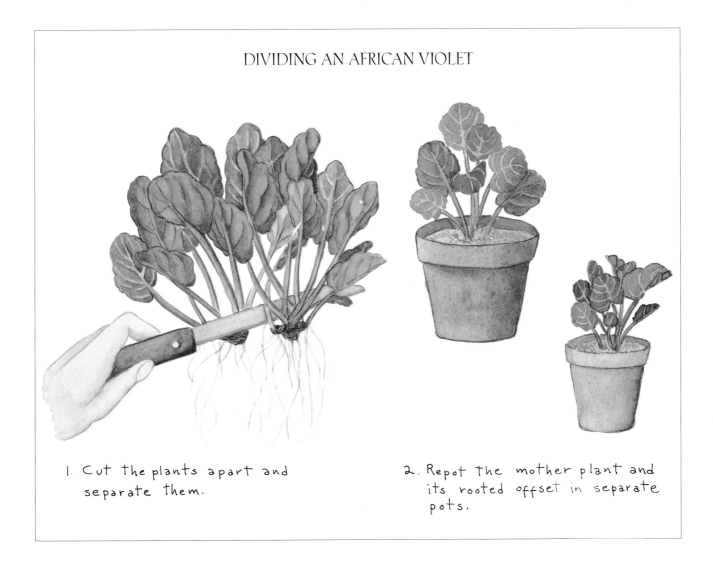

DIVIDING AN AFRICAN VIOLET

1. Cut the plants apart and separate them.

2. Repot the mother plant and its rooted offset in separate pots.

OFFSETS FROM BULBS

Plants that grow from bulbs produce their offsets underground. These are in the form of small new bulbs (*bulblets*).

A bulb is a flat underground stem topped by large scaly leaves that contain stored food. The flower stalk and its green leaves grow from a bud deep in the center of the bulb. Side buds may also develop to form a new bulb next to the old one.

The amaryllis is a spectacular houseplant that sometimes produces bulblets. When its leaves have turned brown and the plant goes into dormancy, take the plant from its container and remove any bulblets before repotting it. Plant each bulblet in its own pot. It may be two or three years before the new bulbs become large enough to flower, so don't get discouraged.

bulblet

amaryllis

cast iron plant

asparagus fern

You can also divide almost any plant that has more than a single stem growing from the compost. The cast iron plant, the asparagus fern, and the umbrella plant are examples. These species gradually fill their pots with a thicket of separate stems that spring up at the soil level. Dividing these plants is more difficult than removing offsets and suckers, because plants that grow in thick clumps do not separate neatly into individual plants.

Once again, you will need an adult helper with a sharp knife to cut down through the root ball. Depending upon the size of the plant, it can be cut into two or more pieces. When the plant is being cut, try to make sure each half or third of the plant comes away with its half or third of the root mass.

Each divided piece can be planted in potting compost in its own container. Water the pots well and keep them out of strong light while they are recovering. It helps to seal each pot in a transparent plastic bag for a few days.

Cuttings

Division, offsets, and the other kinds of vegetative propagation that have been described so far are fairly simple. You merely separate a complete (or nearly complete) new plant from the parent and put it in a pot with compost.

However, new plants can also be started by using small pieces of the parent plant, called cuttings. Many species have the remarkable ability to grow a whole new plant from a piece of stem, a leaf, or even (in some species) a tiny segment of a leaf. A single plant may provide enough cuttings for a whole shelf full of new specimens. This is the most common form of vegetative propagation and the one usually used by commercial growers to increase their stock.

The perfect time to experiment with cuttings is when you want to trim one of your plants to encourage more branching. Get some adult help for this type of propagation, because plant pieces used as cuttings should be cut cleanly rather than pinched off. Most kinds of cuttings are inserted in starting compost immediately, before they lose any moisture. Cacti and plants that ooze with heavy sap after cutting are exceptions: To avoid rotting, they should be left to dry for a day before being set in compost.

The cuttings should be inserted in moist seed-starting compost and their containers enclosed in a transparent plastic bag. Keep the cuttings warm and in good light but out of the sun. When the cuttings root, they are ready for transplanting into potting compost.

Some kinds of cuttings will grow roots even if they are kept in plain water. However, these roots are adapted to absorbing oxygen from water rather than from compost, so the plant may suffer a setback when the rooted cutting is moved to compost.

If you start cuttings in water, move them to compost when the roots are no more than one-fourth of an inch long. At this stage, they can adjust to the change more easily.

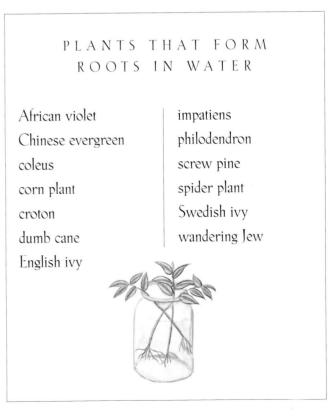

PLANTS THAT FORM
ROOTS IN WATER

African violet	impatiens
Chinese evergreen	philodendron
coleus	screw pine
corn plant	spider plant
croton	Swedish ivy
dumb cane	wandering Jew
English ivy	

Stem Cuttings

Most houseplants can be started from a piece of stem with a few leaves attached. Ornamental figs, geraniums, polka dot plants, peperomias, and wax plants are a few examples. Have your adult helper cut off some branches that are three to five inches long (or shorter, if it is a small plant). The cut should be made just above a leaf (or pair of leaves) on the plant.

The bottom of each cutting should be trimmed off just below its lowest leaves, and any flower buds growing on the stem should be removed. Then pinch off a few of the lowest leaves on the stem, leaving just two or three at the top. If it is a plant with very large leaves, you can cut off the top half of each leaf so the cutting will lose less moisture while it is rooting.

Dip the bottom end of the cutting in rooting hormone and make a hole in the seed-starting compost. Bury the cutting so that only the leafy part is above the level of the compost.

Most stem cuttings will form roots within four to six weeks.

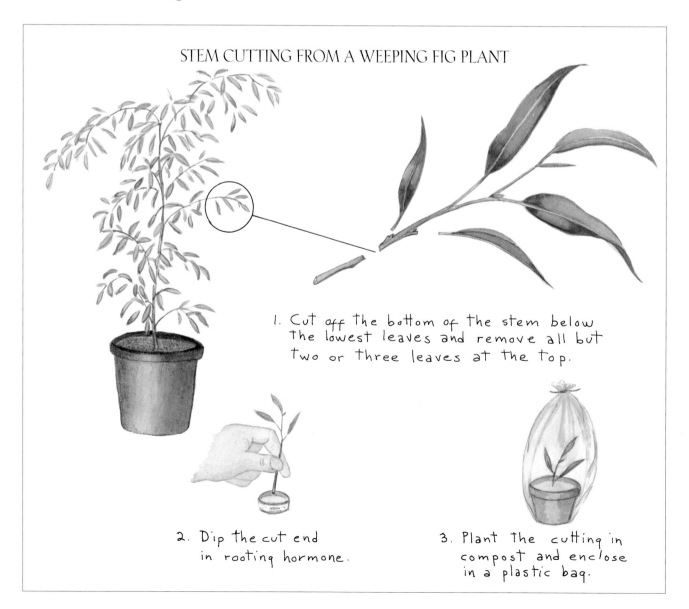

STEM CUTTING FROM A WEEPING FIG PLANT

1. Cut off the bottom of the stem below the lowest leaves and remove all but two or three leaves at the top.

2. Dip the cut end in rooting hormone.

3. Plant the cutting in compost and enclose in a plastic bag.

Cane Cuttings

Chinese evergreen, corn plant, and dumb cane have tough, woody stems called canes. As they grow, their lower leaves are gradually shed, one by one. In time, the plant becomes tall and awkward, a long bare cane with a tuft of leaves on top. These plants are perfect candidates for cuttings.

The leafy top can be removed and propagated as a stem cutting. The bottom of the cane should be cut off three or four inches above the soil line. (Your adult helper may need a pruner or even a small saw to cut the tough stem.) If you keep the plant watered, the stub will sprout new top growth.

If you examine the remaining piece of bare cane, you will see that it has joints all along its length. The stem should be cut into short pieces with at least one joint on each piece. Since Chinese evergreen and dumb cane contain sap that may irritate the skin, you should handle the cut pieces with rubber gloves to be on the safe side. (And don't touch your face or rub your eyes until you have scrubbed away any trace of sap from your gloves or hands.)

Lay the pieces of cane on their sides in starting compost, pressing each one down until it is half-buried, and enclose the container in a plastic bag. On pieces of dumb cane, look between the joints for a small bump, or eye, on the surface of the cane. Like the eye of a potato, this is a dormant growth bud. Place the pieces of dumb cane in the compost with the eye on top.

Unless the cuttings have exactly the right amount of warmth, it may take several months before they produce roots and shoots. When they have at least two leaves, you can remove the bag and transplant them to potting compost.

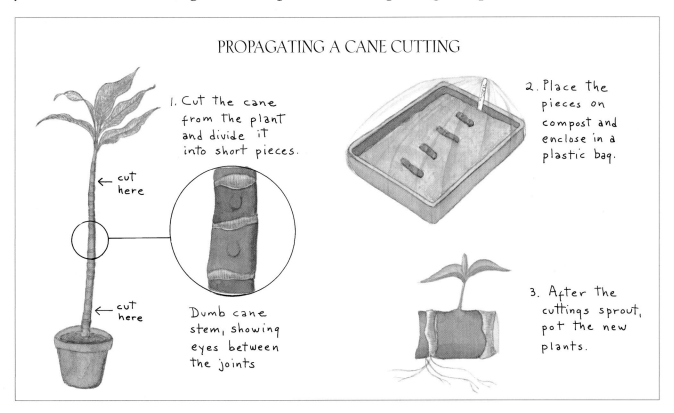

PROPAGATING A CANE CUTTING

1. Cut the cane from the plant and divide it into short pieces.

← cut here

← cut here

Dumb cane stem, showing eyes between the joints

2. Place the pieces on compost and enclose in a plastic bag.

3. After the cuttings sprout, pot the new plants.

Rhizome Cuttings

Some plants have fleshy rhizomes that grow along the surface of the compost. On older plants, the stiff rhizome may extend out beyond the edge of the pot, with its leaves growing up in space. A mature rabbit's foot fern completely covers its container with long hairy rhizomes. Most of the popular rex begonias, with bold markings of silver, cream, pink, red, purple, or copper on their leaves, also have thick rhizomes.

Pieces of rhizome can be used to start new plants. Ask an adult to separate the rhizome from the parent plant with a sharp knife. Then have your helper cut the rhizome into several pieces, each with at least one node. Press each piece into starting compost with the leaf bud on top and enclose the pot in a plastic bag until you see new growth. The parent plant will also send up new growth from the remnant left in its pot.

RHIZOMES

Bulbs (see page 38) and *rhizomes* (RYE-zomes) are unusual stem structures that serve as storage containers for food.

A rhizome is a storage stem growing level with the surface of the soil (or compost) rather than upright. It may grow underground or, especially in the case of potted plants, just above the surface. Like all stems, rhizomes have buds along their length. The buds are usually located at the *nodes*, or joints. Any of these buds is a possible growth point for a new plant.

rhizomes

rabbit's foot fern

PROPAGATING A BEGONIA RHIZOME

nodes

1. Cut the rhizome from the parent plant.

2. Cut off the leafy tip with a piece of rhizome and bury the cut end in a pot of compost.

3. Press the rhizome pieces into another pot of compost. Enclose both pots in plastic bags.

Leaf Cuttings

If you choose the right species of plant, you can even produce new plants from a single leaf.

Here is the method to use for African violets, thick-leaved peperomias, and some begonias, including rex begonias. Choose a mature leaf—but not one of the oldest ones on the plant—and remove it with its petiole (see illustration) attached. You may be able to snap it off cleanly. Otherwise, have an adult cut it from the plant. Dip the cut end in rooting hormone and bury the petiole in starting compost. The leaf blade should not touch the compost. Place the container in a plastic bag. You should see

PARTS OF A LEAF

blade

veins

petiole

miniature plants at the base of each leaf in four to six weeks. Sometimes more than one tiny plant will grow from a leaf. In that case, separate the new plants carefully and plant each in its own small pot.

Jade plant, burro's tail, echeveria, and other succulents have plump leaves with no petioles. Break or cut a few leaves from any of these plants and let the broken ends dry for a day or two before inserting them in starting compost. Keep the compost moist until new roots and shoots grow from the leaves. These leaves are not in danger of drying out, so the container does not need to be covered with a plastic bag.

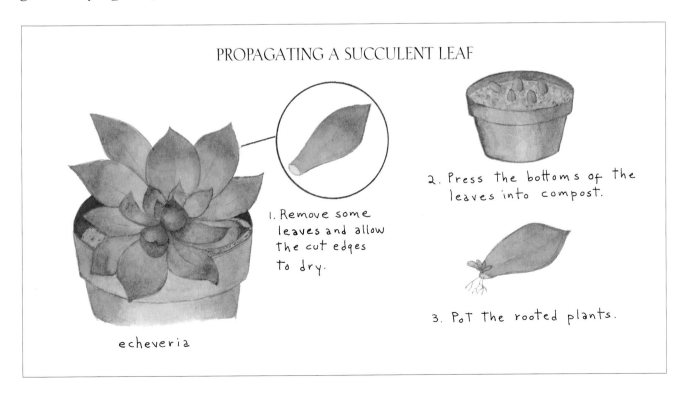

PROPAGATING A SUCCULENT LEAF

1. Remove some leaves and allow the cut edges to dry.

2. Press the bottoms of the leaves into compost.

3. Pot the rooted plants.

echeveria

Leaf Segments

You can even grow new plants from a mere sliver of a leaf. Try this with a heavily veined leaf from a rex begonia.

First make sure that your tools, compost, and containers are absolutely clean, because pieces cut from a leaf are subject to rotting. Slice a begonia leaf into six or seven wedge-shaped pieces, making sure that a vein runs through each piece and that the heavier end of the vein is at the pointed tip of the wedge. Insert the points in the starting compost and handle them just like other cuttings.

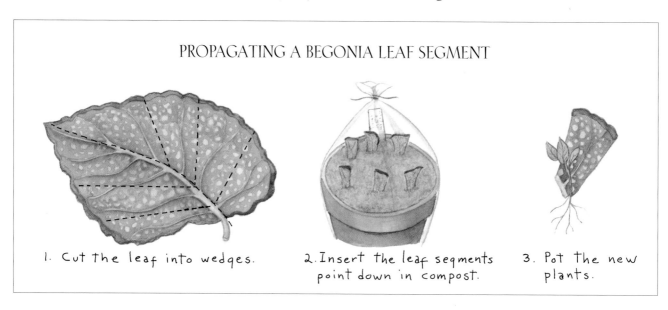

PROPAGATING A BEGONIA LEAF SEGMENT

1. Cut the leaf into wedges.

2. Insert the leaf segments point down in compost.

3. Pot the new plants.

Snake plants perform the same trick but with one difference: If you use a leaf with yellow stripes along its edges, the plants that grow from the segments will probably not have this pattern. (If you want a new plant with the same striped markings, you can get it by dividing the parent plant. See pages 37–39.)

For best results, try this in the summertime. Cut the long leaves into two-inch segments. Cut the top of each segment on an angle, so you will be able to tell the top from the bottom. Let the cut surfaces dry overnight. Then press the *lower* (unangled) end of each piece halfway into starting compost. Do not enclose these cuttings in plastic.

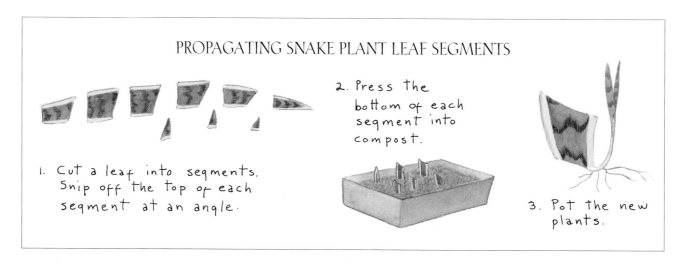

PROPAGATING SNAKE PLANT LEAF SEGMENTS

1. Cut a leaf into segments. Snip off the top of each segment at an angle.

2. Press the bottom of each segment into compost.

3. Pot the new plants.

44

In a month or so, when you see a new plant growing, remove it from the compost. Cut away the original leaf segment and pot the new plant.

For more information about growing new plants from old, check the books at your local library. Some of them provide specific directions for propagating many different kinds of plants.

Even if you are not sure about what method to use for the plants you own, don't be afraid to experiment. After all, the risk isn't great. If a whole pot of cuttings fails to take root, try to figure out the reasons for failure. And remember, you still have the original plant, so nothing keeps you from trying again.

If you succeed, you receive a double reward: the satisfaction of using your new gardening skills, and a shelf full of young plants for your windowsill garden.

Trial and error is a great teacher, and you will learn something from each experience. As your confidence and gardening skill grow, you may want to try your hand with some of the more demanding species of plants. Indoor gardeners never run out of challenges. It is a hobby that can give pleasure for a lifetime!

C O M M O N   H O U S E P L A N T S

The abbreviation *spp.,* appearing after the name of a plant genus, stands for the plural form of the word *species. Echinocactus spp.,* for example, designates all species in the genus *Echinocactus.*

When the air is dry, plants needing increased humidity or high humidity will be helped by pebble trays; plants requiring high humidity will profit from additional moisture, such as frequent misting.

PLANT NAME	LIGHT	SPECIAL CARE	HOW TO PROPAGATE
African violet *Saintpaulia hybrida*	Medium	Increased humidity	Division, leaf cuttings
aloe *Aloe spp.*	Bright	Prefers low humidity	Stem cuttings, offsets
aluminum plant *Pilea cadierei*	Medium	Pinch back often	Stem cuttings
amaryllis *Hippeastrum hybrida*	Bright during active growth	No water in dormancy	Bulb offsets
asparagus fern *Asparagus densiflorus*	Medium to bright, no strong sun		Division
avocado *Persea americana*	Bright	Pinch back to encourage branching	Seed
baby's tears *Helxine soleirolii*	Medium	Prefers high humidity	Division
barrel cactus *Echinocactus spp.* See cactus, desert types			
begonia *Begonia spp.*	Medium for most, bright for flowering species	Increased humidity	Cuttings of stem, rhizome, leaf, leaf segments
Boston fern *Nephrolepis exaltata*	Medium	Increased humidity	Division
burro's tail *Sedum morganianum*	Bright	Fragile; leaves detach easily	Stem cuttings, individual leaves
cactus desert types	Bright	Minimum water in fall and winter	Stem cuttings, offsets
forest types	Medium	Keep cool and water lightly in dormancy	Stem cuttings
cast iron plant *Aspidistra elatior*	Medium to low, no direct sun		Division
chenille plant *Acalypha hispida*	Bright	High humidity	Stem cuttings
Chinese evergreen *Aglaonema modestum*	Low to medium	High humidity; needs warmth	Division, stem cuttings
Christmas cactus *Schlumbergera bridgesii* See cactus, forest types			
coleus *Coleus blumei*	Bright	Keep pinching back	Seeds, stem cuttings
corn plant *Dracena fragrans*	Medium	Prefers high humidity	Stem or cane cuttings
croton *Codiaeum variegatum*	Bright	High humidity	Stem cuttings
crown of thorns *Euphorbia milii*	Bright	Prefers low humidity	Stem cuttings
cyclamen *Cyclamen persicum*	Bright to medium during active growth	No water during dormancy	Seeds
dumb cane *Dieffenbachia spp.*	Medium	Prefers high humidity	Stem or cane cuttings
echeveria *Echeveria spp.*	Bright	Prefers dry air	Leaf cuttings
English ivy *Hedera helix*	Bright to medium	Increased humidity	Stem cuttings
fig *Ficus spp.*	Bright to medium	Increased humidity	Stem cuttings (for nonwoody stems)
fishhook cactus *Ferrocactus latispinus* See cactus, desert types			
geranium *Pelargonium spp.*	Bright		Seeds, stem cuttings
heart-leaved philodendron *Philodendron scandens* See philodendron			
impatiens *Impatiens spp.*	Bright	Flowers best when crowded in pot; water often	Seeds, stem cuttings
jade plant *Crassula argentea*	Bright	Prefers dry air	Stem or leaf cuttings
kalanchoe *Kalanchoe blossfeldiana*	Bright		Stem or leaf cuttings

kangaroo vine *Cissus antarctica*	Bright	Climber; needs support	Stem cuttings
lemon *Citrus limon*	Bright		Seeds
mother-of-thousands *Kalanchoe daigremontiana*	Bright		Plantlets
nerve plant *Fittonia spp.*	Medium to low	Needs high humidity	Stem cuttings
orchid cactus *Epiphyllum spp.* *See* cactus, forest types			
partridge breast aloe *Aloe variegata* *See* aloe			
peace lily *Spathyphyllum spp.*	Medium	High humidity	Division
peperomia *Peperomia spp.*	Medium	Increased humidity	Stem or leaf cuttings
petunia *Petunia hybrida*	Bright	Pick off old flowers	Seeds
philodendron *Philodendron spp.*	Medium to low, no direct sun	Supports for climbing species	Layering, stem cuttings
piggyback plant *Tolmiea menziesii*	Medium		Plantlets
poinsettia *Euphorbia pulcherrima*	Bright	Needs special care for second-year bloom	Stem cuttings in summer
polka dot plant *Hypoestes phyllostachya*	Bright	Increased humidity; pinch back often	Stem cuttings
pothos *Epipremnum spp.*	Medium	Climber; pinch back for bushiness	Stem cuttings
prayer plant *Maranta leuconeura*	Medium	Increased humidity	Division
rabbit's foot fern *Davillia fejeensis*	Medium	Prefers high humidity	Rhizome cuttings
rex begonia *Begonia rex* *See* begonia			
rubber plant *Ficus elastica* *See* fig			
schefflera *Brassaia actinophylla*	Bright to medium	Keep leaves clean	Stem cuttings (difficult)
screw pine *Pandanus veitchii*	Medium	High humidity	Offsets
sea urchin cactus *Echinopsis rhodotricha* *See* cactus, desert types			
shamrock plant *Oxalis deppei*	Bright	Overgrown plants become leggy and need dividing	Division
snake plant *Sansevieria trifasciata*	Bright to low	Avoid overwatering	Offsets, division, leaf segments
spider plant *Chlorophytum comosum*	Medium to bright		Plantlets, division
strawberry begonia *Saxifraga stolonifera*	Bright	Increased humidity	Plantlets
Swedish ivy *Plectranthus oertendahlii*	Medium	Pinch back to encourage bushiness	Stem cuttings
sweet potato *Ipomoea batatas*	Bright	Grow in compost or water	Tuber (whole potato), stem cuttings
ti plant *Cordyline terminalis*	Bright to medium	Increased humidity	Offsets, cane cuttings
umbrella plant *Cyperus alternifolius*	Bright to medium	Keep soil moist to wet	Division
wandering Jew *Tradescantia fluminensis*	Bright to medium	High humidity	Stem cuttings
watermelon peperomia *Peperomia argyreia* *See* peperomia			
wax begonia *Begonia semperflorens* *See* begonia			
wax plant *Hoya carnosa*	Bright	Prefers high humidity	Layering, stem cuttings
weeping fig *Ficus benjamina* *See* fig			

INDEX OF PLANTS

Illustrations are in **boldface.**